Under the Sign of the Lily

The Messianic Sophianic Age

The Curtain Falls

The Sword of Damocles Over the Two Swords of Church and State

*The Eternal Word,
the One God, the Free Spirit,
speaks through Gabriele,
as through all the prophets of God—
Abraham, Job, Moses, Elijah, Isaiah,
Jesus of Nazareth,
the Christ of God*

The Curtain Falls

The Sword of Damocles Over the Two Swords of Church and State

The Cherub of the Divine Wisdom
and God-Father, the Eternal All-One,
gave revelations in April 2021
through the prophetess and
emissary of God, Gabriele

Gabriele
Publishing House

"The Curtain Falls
The Sword of Damocles Over the Two Swords
of Church and State"

1st Edition, February 2024
© Gabriele-Verlag Das Wort GmbH
Max-Braun-Str. 2, 97828 Marktheidenfeld
www.gabriele-verlag.com
www.gabriele-publishing-house.com

Translated from the original German title:

„Der Vorhang fällt
Das Damoklesschwert über den zwei Schwerten
Von Kirche und Staat"

The German edition is the work of reference
for all questions regarding the meaning of the contents.

Order No. S 195EN

All decorative letters: © Gabriele-Verlag Das Wort

Printed by: KlarDruck GmbH, Marktheidenfeld, Germany

ISBN 978-3-96446-422-4

Table of Contents

Preface

For nearly five decades, heaven, the Eternal Kingdom of God, the Eternal Being, has been open, because the Eternal Kingdom has given and continues to give to humankind from the cornucopia of divine Wisdom, spiritual-divine teachings from the Sanctum of Being—in the prophetic word for the present time and for future generations. The eternal Father-Mother-God, His Son, the Christ of God, and the Prince of divine Wisdom before the throne of God have given revelations in an unprecedented fullness.

This time, this unique cosmic event—which will never come again—is gradually drawing to a close.

Read the following revelation from the divine Wisdom and the Call of the Eternal All-One to His sons and daughters in earthly garment.

The Curtain Falls

The Sword of Damocles Over the
Two Swords of Church and State

O nce more, the Wisdom of God introduces itself. Together, Cherub and Seraph are the supporting pair of the third basic power of the one primordial eternal law, God:

I, the Cherub, the law-prince of the divine Wisdom in the spirit, and the Seraph, my dual, my spiritual wife, who is still in an earthly body called Gabriele, the prophetess of God, the same as the interpreter of the word of God, of the Eternal Kingdom.

In unity with the third basic power of God, the eternal primordial law before the throne of God, the other six law-princes with their duals, that is, seven regencies, work on behalf of the Almighty One God of the love for God and neighbor.

*T*he topic of "The Curtain Falls" is about an immense millionfold, even billionfold, debt, or burden, which a phalanx of violence has burdened itself with in relation to its countless victims and the eternal law of love for God and neighbor, and about the time of the Fall-regime that is coming to an end.

As the curtain falls, the actors introduce themselves.

The Fall from the Kingdom of God was started by several divine beings who had stipulated that they wanted to shape the eternal creation, the "Let there be" of the Creator, in a different way.

From the All-One, the Creator of infinity, who, with the seven primordial forces, had initiated, discussed, developed and in long cycles created and set in motion the "Let there be" in all details, the Fall-beings requested a considerable amount of energy, that is, drawing and creating Light Ether, in order to prove to the Eternal All-One, how His creation could be better arranged. The *quantum of Light Ether was also given to them by the Eternal as a loan—mind you, as a loan.*

With these immeasurable energetic, drawing and creating light-etheric energies upon energies, they left the Eternal Kingdom of love and unity and drew a so-called wall of light with counter-reflection over certain energetic poles, in order to feel separate from the Eternal Kingdom.

Without taking into account the All-Law of "like attracts like"—that is: all the same behavior patterns attract one another, duplicate and rein-force one another—the Fall-beings began to cre-ate their realms and to develop their own ideas of how they wanted to conceptualize their "Let there be."

Already with the first distribution of the loan, that is, of the considerable quantum of Light Ether, the first disagreements began, in terms of who was the greatest in which etheric area, be-cause the one wanted it to be different than the other.

It did not take long, and then the division be-gan, which means: In the fine-material energies, the Light Ether, which they took with them and distributed as a superabundant energy of drawing and creating power, already the first traces of condensation of the energetic Light Ether became visible, which means: to become coarser in the overall structure. In their eagerness over who could be the greatest, the Fall-beings hardly noticed that they spun themselves more and more into so-called energetic layers, also called spinning nebulas, which became more and more dense and likewise more impenetrable.

To indicate the whole Fall-system just briefly, I, the Cherub of His Wisdom, through the instrument of God, Gabriele, give a revelation in only general terms about cosmic systems and about cosmic passages, and also about cosmoses left behind. Galaxies over galaxies, solar systems over solar systems, planets over planets—all borrowed divine energies—are also mentioned here only briefly.

The mass of borrowed energy overwhelmed the Fall-beings, whereby from the very beginning, everyone wanted to be the greatest. Soon after, the Fall-beings separated from one another. Every separation, which had within its respective arbitrary will, led to a self-appointed system of rulers, of course, with gods and goddesses.

From system to system, spoken with today's words, from state structures to state structures, they fell and enveloped themselves with their own desires and feelings, which were, and are, nothing other than energies of the Fall.

As stated: The Cherub of His Wisdom, who I am, gives here only a very broad overview and insight into the becoming all the way to becoming human.

Over countless times, from Fall to Fall, the formerly pure, fine-material divine beings, the spirit beings, became Fall-beings with ever denser, heavier and more massive forms, up to becoming human, that is, the coarse-material human being, who now consists of bones, veins, muscles, that is, of flesh. Today, one calls the deepest state of the Fall-system "matter."

To the Fall-phalanx, which had to leave whole cosmoses again and again, because these could no longer support them on account of their continuing condensation, messengers from the Eternal Kingdom, God, came again and again. They were and are until today constantly striving to reveal to their brothers and sisters the path back into the Eternal Kingdom.

Through the changes of their personal desires, the Fall-beings —and that, into the present time—always drew new hope that they could defeat the Eternal One, that is, His Eternal Word.

Since the Fall-energy became ever denser and finally, became matter, only one planet exists that is habitable for them, called Earth.

The low point of today is the proof: the fight of one against the other to hold land and estates, property and goods according to their respective ideas. The many tyrants of the various systems, each of whom had their own gods, goddesses and alleged "saints," were so at odds with each other that they all believed they could defeat the others with battle tirades, which to this day they have not succeeded in doing.

If help from the Kingdom of God—God's messengers, God's prophets and God's prophetesses—came to the Fall-beings, then it was either: "Keep silent and disappear" or "We will silence you," which the Fall-beings also carried out. Always, only fighting, violence and murder.

The first messengers of God who came to the renegade beings from the Kingdom of God still had the possibility to retreat via certain planetary radiations in order to return to the Eternal Kingdom of God. Once the condensation increased and this safe return to the Kingdom of God was no longer possible, the fight against the messengers of God continued, by which they were persecuted, slandered, beaten or even slain. It continued with cruel torture and execution with various cruel instruments of murder. From system to system, that is, from Fall to Fall, the so-called gods and their subordinates became more aggressive and brutal.

The fratricide, the slaying, execution and killing, started already with the first wave of the bestial Fall-systems. From Fall-system to Fall-system, each state power had its gods and so-called saints that they worshipped.

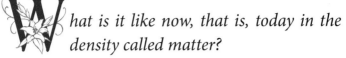

hat is it like now, that is, today in the density called matter?

Every state power has its idol. Until today, this belief in gods prevails; until today, every person— the one more, the other less—has their idols, their images of gods.

One, who wants to rule over everyone and over everything, is the idol and god of blood sacrifice Baal with those servile to him. Right into the present time, the "god" Baal has had different names and symbols and still has influence on governments and nations.

Into a system of domination with two swords as a signet, nearly five decades ago, came a momentous writing with far-reaching content for the receiver, who immediately, without checking it out, set in motion, as usual, the church and state inquisitorial eradication detachment. The law-prince of the divine Wisdom announced the workings of the prophetess of God—a woman— to the power-holders of the worldly religious constructs, the "churches."

As stated, it did not take long, and another part of the Baalistic curtain opened, and hundreds of actors entered the world stage of the Inquisition Theater of the present time. They began to act according to their own mindset, without ethics and with the lowest morals.

First, came the flood of slander with lies and threats, and then, the concealed attempt to lock the prophetess of God in a cage and let her express—unheard by people—what God had to say through her. On the one hand, these speculative thoughts and accusations did not go down well with the free human being, Gabriele. On the other hand, the incarnated Seraph of the divine Wisdom was and is completely underestimated, as is, above all, also the protection from the Kingdom of God by the seven Cherubim before God's throne.

The present-day goverment was also put into action; after all, it has to obey the two swords, in that the one serves the other, of course, always under the rule of the church.

The fight against the word of the Free Spirit, of the eternal All-One Creator-God, continued with ever dirtier slogans of lies, no matter whether it came from pastors, priests, provincial politicians, career-addicted provincial journalists or the incited people.

As it once was, so it is today. The accusations were hardly distinguishable from the times before this time, always accompanied by the cry: "They should be hanged and slaughtered!"—Thus, for example, the cry of a village mob stirred up by priests and pastors.

The theological side in a cleverly covered state carousel silently hoped that the agitation of the priests and pastors and the unrestrained inquisitorial clamor of their faithful among the people intoxicated by incense, would set in motion the murderous fruit of the inquisitorial thought, as so often during the centuries and millennia.

The old, already dilapidated curtain no longer closed. Despite all the tricks and skills—the old, musty curtain remained open, and the actors became more and more visible without their masquerades.

One is amazed: Via church and state, two swords are ready for use by both the church and state.

The unatoned inquisitorial crimes of past times rang in the ears of the present time. As stated: The gullible, incited citizens cried: "Hang them up, down with the riffraff, they should be snuffed out!" and much more.

The two swords of state and church did not come into effect, because, for one thing, the Cherub stood behind his Seraph, the prophetess of God, and not lastly, the other six spiritual-cosmic Cherubim: energetic powers that before the throne of God are responsible for the primordial law of the Eternal Kingdom.

he times of times are changing; they are coming to an end. The announcement, the coming of the Christ of God has been spoken, the Fall-number "from—to" is approaching its end, the overloaded and overburdened world-ship is gradually going under.

To repeat: No moaning as well as no hoarding of riches will help—the world-ship is sinking.

On this Earth, in this world, there is much talk of the times, also of the "time." Thus, humankind goes with the time. This means: from—to, for example, from morning at 7:00 o'clock to midday at 1:00 o'clock. Therefore, time is decisive. It sets the pace, for example, it says: "The person is still young," or "the person is already older or old." In each situation, time is decisive, it plays a considerable role. People also speak of time that has run out, or even: "The clock stood still; it's already later," etc., etc. But it's always about time.

Time is energy! Who can calculate the energies of the times?

The Cherub of His divine Wisdom before the throne of God goes several large steps further with the question: What is eternity?

Can eternity run out? Does it have a time limit?

Many people say they haven't thought about it yet. Another thinks: "Eternity is, simply, eternity!" Still others say: "Only a theologian could give an answer to this or a scientist!"

Does the scientist have knowledge concerning "eternity," or does he create knowledge—whereby the basis of the knowledge has so many terms and words that he himself and the listeners no longer know what the result is, with all the ifs and buts. Well, eternity remains simply eternity, without time and space.

Another overriding question could be: Who can tell us human beings what eternity means?

Perhaps, the seven Cherubim and Seraphim before the throne of the Almighty, the law-guardians of eternity, who were only briefly mentioned here? However, to understand this, an interpretor, a translator is needed, for one can imagine that eternity has another basis for its language.

The Cherub of the third basic power of God provides the answer: In eternity the language of unity is the law of the love for God and neighbor. That sounds so plain and simple: "love for God and neighbor."

Does humankind from the times of times, from generation to generation, know at all, why God, the Eternal, sent very many prophets and prophetesses of God, as well as other proclaimers of God? Because divine beings from the Kingdom of God, from eternity, live the eternal law, the love for God and neighbor, and in this spirit, communicate with all Being, for this is the language of eternity. It is the All-communication.

This world, all the countries on this Earth, have their cultural philosophy and their specific language, which respectively needs its translators.

To give human beings an understanding of the language of the eternal law of love for God and neighbor, beings from the eternal Being incarnated again and again and became human beings. They came to give the Eternal Word of unity, the law of the love for God and neighbor, in the respective local language of the incarnated being, which was now a human being.

Hardly anyone thinks about incarnation, about why there is a human body only briefly, which dies today, and that tomorrow another will be born—and why "another"?

The person supposes: "Time is simply time, which holds true for each person." If that is true, then what sense would eternity have?

If people would ask themselves: "What is time," then they would go further with the question: Where does time come from, since everything is supposed to be infinite eternity, and thus, without space and time?

God spoke: "Let there be light"—and there was light. The Eternal did not speak of shadow.

The question stands: Where does time come from, ultimately, the time of day, figuratively speaking, also the seasons, according to which humankind orients itself?

Many people deduce the time from the position of the sun. The logical answer is therefore: from the position of the sun.

Why can't the sun shine through the Earth? Because the Earth is simply the Earth and not permeable. It is just solid substance, matter. One could also say: It is just not permeable. The question stands: Why not? Secular science certainly knows the answer. When it comes to the "why," why the Earth is solid, science can surely unravel the knot.

When it also is a question of time, it surely has the answer, even if it is the big bang, whereby it is assumed that density, that is, matter, and life on Earth emerged as a result.

What is the meaning of eternity—time—life?

Briefly considered: Eternity is simply eternity, without beginning and end. Time, however, would have to have a beginning and an end.

Another question: Whoever created the beginning of time—they should also have determined the end of time, shouldn't they?

Questions after questions …

Who created human beings and the animals, and who determines the death of the individual human being and who, the death of the animals?

Who created the sun, the moon and the stars, and who created the seasons?

Why do the planets revolve in certain orbits around the sun?

Who created the types of atoms and the quanta?

Who or what is this Intelligence, which permeates everything according to iron laws and wisely arranged it all?

Are the cosmic principles of the law pure coincidence, or is a cosmic Intelligence behind them?

What is light? What is space? What is time? All coincidence?

Questions after questions—who has the answer?

od, the Eternal, gave answers through His proclaimers, called prophets and prophetesses. Many of them were persecuted and murdered by the world luminaries of emperors, kings, priests and religious leaders—to continue the whole thing with the "two swords" and the clerical power—or they were slandered and then hushed up, in order to pay homage to the Moloch principle, and this, at all times, with all the associated honors on the part of church and state, including the corresponding goods and funds, and this, until today.

At all times these were and are the characteristics of the two swords and of the clerical power: slander, intrigues, character assassination, fighting, dispute, war, murder and genocide, also the most malicious lies; it continued with exclusions, disadvantages of so-called "others," formerly called heretics, on all levels where state and church assert their influence wherever possible, up to countless unsuspecting families, where it came to separation due to defamation, agitation and smear campaigns.

Only destruction, wherever one looks. At all times it was and is the rotten fruits of those faithful to Baal in cassocks and regalia.

What did Jesus, the Christ, say?

"You will recognize them by their fruit. Are grapes gathered from thorn bushes, or figs from thistles?

Every healthy tree bears good fruit, but the diseased tree bears bad fruit.

A healthy tree cannot bear bad fruit, nor can a diseased tree bear good fruit. Every tree that does not bear good fruit is cut down and thrown into the fire.

Thus, you will recognize them by their fruit. Not everyone who says to me, 'Lord, Lord,' will enter the kingdom of heaven, but the one who does the will of my Father who is in heaven. On that day many will say to me, 'Lord, Lord, did we not prophesy in your name, and cast out demons in your name, and do many mighty works in your name?' And then will I declare to them, 'I

never knew you; depart from me, you who prac-
tice lawlessness.'"

The shadows of time give answer:
Who planted the good tree and who, the bad
one?
Who is eternity and who is time?
Who had the proclaimers of God, the proph-
ets and prophetesses, murdered? And why? What
for? How come?

herefore, everything has its time—except
for eternity, which hardly anyone can tell
you about. And why not?
Eternity is All-eternal! The primordial eternal
Spirit of truth spoke: Let there be light! Let there
be a primordial eternal kingdom! And it was!
The mighty "Let there be" is the All-Spirit, the
infinite law of the eternal Being, God's love, from
which the fine-material, forming Eternal King-
dom emerged, which is seven-dimensional. The

first beings, the first dual pairs, came into being. The four units of drawing and creating, the cradle of the filiation of God, came into being. In the book "The Age of the Lily, Sophia, the Wisdom of God—the Spirit of Truth, the Spirit of Fusion: Spirit of His Spirit, Love of His Love," more can be read about this. Viewed all in all, it is the eternity.

As often revealed: This and much more can be read in the Sophia Library, the Center of the Free Spirit.

Where does time come from, since time is always conditional? Time did not come from God, the Eternal, the Father-Mother-God, because God is eternity, the primordial eternal law of the love for God and neighbor. Nor did time come from the seven guardians of the law, the Cherubim and Seraphim.

Anyone who has read about the fusion of the seven primordial energies has an inkling of this. The fusion of the primordial energies indicates the "Let there be," the eternal, energetic, primordial stream of eternity, the "Let there be," the Being in the Being. That is why eternity is simply eternity.

Let it be repeated: The divine beings came and come forth from the divine law of love for God and neighbor, Being that became form. The "Let there be," the Being, is drawing and creating power, God, the Father-Mother-God and His sons and daughters.

There is more to read about the eternal law, the Being in the Being, in the book: "The Age of the Lily—Sophia, the Wisdom of God. The Four Planes of Development, the Cradle of Evolution to the Filiation of God."

Eternity, the Being, is constant evolution, constant giving and receiving in the primordial stream of the Being. Through this, every divine being, that is, spirit being, is Being that became form, eternity that became form.

Eternity is all-encompassing Being. The eternal Being, eternity, can also be seen as the law of unity. It is the law of the love for God and neighbor.

*P*articularly when it comes to the word "eternity," I, the Cherub of eternal Wisdom, would like to keep repeating some things through my dual, the Seraph, who is still in the human body to interpret the message of heaven, because it is, after all, about eternity, the law of the love for God and neighbor.

Seen as a whole: The Being is eternity, and in the Being, the divine beings are Being that became form, beings of eternity, eternity that became form.

Since the Fall of several beings, who wanted to arrange the "Let there be," the eternal Being, differently, there exists a transformation of light, like a wall of light, around the Eternal Kingdom.

Who wanted to separate the Being in the Being and made the corresponding attempt? This can be read among other things in the books "I Am the Christ of God—I Come Soon" and "The Men's World—Yesterday and Today. The Three Attributes of the Father-Mother God and the Capitulation of the Satanist." Therefore, it is the one who *wanted things differently, and wanted to fashion this world, which emerged from his coercive will, differently. Until the present time, he has imposed and imposes his will on this world and influences those who, according to his will, did and do what amounts to what this world is until today, and this, as stated, under his influence.*

After countless times of times, the ruler of the Fall of the times, marked by all imaginable cruelties, gave up his fight and admitted his defeat. In the eternal Sanctum of God, and in the presence of the other six law-princes, he handed over his scepter—like the ruler's staff of his power—to the prince of Wisdom, thus capitulating before the throne of God.

This world, all world regimes, no matter of which color, regardless of which ruler status, or of which form of state or government, are thus at an end. Time, which means "from—to," has expired, it is at its end! All the states of this world, all governments and church gods are in the process of passing away. Whether people live in poverty or

*hoard wealth, whether idolatry or other misbe-
lief, whether the jubilation of victory or song of
lamentation, whether combat or quarrel—any
hubris, everything dries up like a once mighty
stream to which no more energy flows, because it
was merely a loan from the eternal Being.*

*All negative energies are in the process of pass-
ing away, energies that wanted to prove to God,
the Eternal, that it is not the law of unity, the
love for God and neighbor, that is eternal, but
violence, fighting, quarreling, war, manslaughter,
murder, rape of women, abuse of children and
young people, the eradication of whole peoples
and, not to forget, the persecution and murder
of the innumerable emissaries of God, the prophets and prophetesses of God, and, not least, of the
Son of God, who came into this world as Jesus of
Nazareth to defeat the abominable battle-god of
the underworld in the garb of religions and his
priests, who gave himself many names, such as
the "god" Baal, and who, until today, did not hes-
itate to misuse the name of God, the Eternal, and
of His Son Christ for his dissolute purposes.*

He believed that with the threatening conduct of the two swords of church and state, by intimidating, by stirring up fears and by exercising the cruelest, bloodiest violence and the most deviant torture, he could bring everything under his clerical tyranny. The two swords of church and state were to be the clerical sign of violence, the sign of victory against the statement of Jesus of Nazareth: "The one who fights with the sword will perish by the sword."

Very gradually, the fallacy, the hubris of church and state to conquer the world with their two swords, their clerical power, comes to light.

The question stands: Who defeats whom?

Who thinks they can defeat whom? The churches that display the cross with corpus in churches, halls and fields?

The countries that have appropriated the trademark of "Christian values" with an arsenal of weapons coming from so-called "Christian countries"?

Who will be victorious?

The supposed heroes in state and church, the money and wealth as a sign of power? Who?

Everything is not only sinking, in a once-powerful despotic stream of rulers in church and state, which believed it would be able to dominate everything, including the true eternal All-One God, who sent His prophets and God-filled men and women. And nothing, but nothing at all, remains of those either, who established themselves temporarily in the times of times as the idolatrous hegemony and idolatrous mighty, setting their murderous signs through their primitive, violent rulership, when and where it was at all possible for them. Nor does anything remain of the peoples who barbarically wrecked havoc under the spell of the two swords.

Nothing, but absolutely nothing, will remain, not even the power-hungry in cassocks and robes, in regalia or gowns, the wolves in sheep's clothing, the despots and tyrants, the eminences and excellencies who still have something corresponding to say in church and state, and who show their two swords, with the attendant soldiers in the background of their alleged "Christian values."

The stream, the time, is drying up. The end of time brings out everything; therefore, the collapse of time is also called the "end-time" or "climate change," whereby the end-time always goes before in the changing of time, even if the end-time is called "climate change."

Eternity is eternity. Time is simply the end-time, the beginning and end. Just as time comes to an end according to the will of the Eternal All-One God, the peaceable time begins, the New Era, which His divine Wisdom, the third basic power before His throne, announced in the prophetic word. How it continues stands solely in the course of time, just as eternity dictates, solely in the primordial eternal law, the law of eternity, of the love for God and neighbor.

The love for God and neighbor is, as stated, the primordial eternal law, which radiates from the Sanctum of Being and, potentiated, continues to radiate into the fullness. The primordial eternal streaming law took hold of time because the time of the loan is expired. The energies, the "times," have no more inflow. The loan "time" has expired. For better understanding, one could also think of the following picture: The connection to your power grid is interrupted; what is still stored as energy will be used up—then it is over.

The elapsed time could also be compared with a mighty millenia-long, or even billion-year-long, wide stream. When nothing more flows into a mighty stream, the rest runs out or gradually seeps away. And if we take a closer look at the word "end-time," it means that time has come to an end and, as stated, the rest runs out or seeps away.

What does it look like in the many countries of this Earth? Wherever one looks, everywhere there is an ever-increasing disastrous discord.

In terms of the word "energy," this means in the end, because it is about energy, and thus, about time: The so-called governments of all countries come more and more into a crisis as to how they can lead or manipulate the people or even keep them in check. The reins of millennia, or even billions of years, have become brittle. The threatening messages of the religions in the western world with their often state-subsidized ecclesiastical institutions hardly help anymore to keep the people submissive.

And the vengeful god, the idolatrous god, the cult god, has hardly any more influence on the masses. He has served his time.

Wherever one looks in the times over times: Since the Fall-system, Baal, the vengeful god, has been at work with varying names—fighting, quarreling, one against the other, war and genocide, eviction from property and land, fraud, theft, robbery and murder, and always the oppression and plundering of the people for the purposes and goals of the powerful in state and religions. Since the Fall-event, Baal, the vengeful god, the idolatrous god, has been active.

But the goings-on of the Fall are now merely a goings-on conditioned by time. With the activity of the Fall-beings, the loan "time," the same as energy, has become a demonic fire that is dying out, for time is simply conditioned by time. The surrender of the demon becomes more and more visible. To all contrary earthly efforts may be replied: The Christ of God prepares His appearance.

o make understandable what this means: "The time is ripe, the demonic fire is dying out," I, the Cherub of His Wisdom, repeat in the name of the Eternal All-One God:

For nearly five decades, the Eternal All-One and His Son, the Christ of God, have been giving revelations through the messenger of God, that is, the prophetess, Gabriele.

For nearly five decades, I, the Cherub of His Wisdom, have accompanied the instrument of God, Gabriele, who is the incarnated Seraph of divine Wisdom, my dual.

Looking back, let it be said: Four decades have passed since I, the Cherub, addressed the pope at that time and the bishops of both ecclesiastical denominations, through the revelation of a message inspired by me, that God, the Eternal, once again sent a prophet to the Earth, this time a woman.

In my revelation, I denounced the conduct of the rich ecclesiastical institutions, including that of the guilds of priests and pastors, and especially the arrogance they accumulate day after day with the steed, the state, in order to use the spurs on it—of course, for ecclesiastical purposes, mainly for specific "priestly purposes."

I revealed that it is "advisable to bow down before the One God who is the life in all things." To realize this requires neither priests nor pastors, neither churches nor state funds.

Soon after this message to the pope of that time, to the bishops of both denominations, the fight against the word of God of the present time began, without listening to the Christ of God, to what He has to say through His instrument, because the Kingdom of God does not have the language of human beings.

As usual, lies and the most malicious slander were the order of the day, which was to bring, and partly did bring, strife and destruction to families that initially were still intact, according to the well-tried inquisitorial pattern. The years-long inquisitorial running of the gauntlet in the church-servile media landscape of the state and the media owned by the churches was intended— as at all times—above all, to stir up the people, which also soon bore fruit, for it was all about finishing off the followers of Jesus of Nazareth, "those unsavory characters of an alien caste of mind," which might also have succeeded if a Protestant pastor had not suddenly and unexpectedly fallen victim to his own inflammatory slogans.

Both ecclesiastical institutions were and are until today, the agitators, and the state, faithful to them, sees to hushing up the present word of God through the mouth of prophets until today, 2021, according to the doctrine of the two swords.

But as it is written: What a person sows, the person will reap—an eye for an eye, a tooth for a tooth.

In retrospect, more and more people can understand why the state, the state steed, is silent— after all, it is one with the ecclesiastical power, with the two swords that symbolize state and church. Both swords are in the power of the church, thus, the state is under the rod of the church—and ultimately, also the soldiers who have to fight for state and church.

The state talks about democracy! How can this be? Who determines: church or state?

Well, the curtain of the millennia, if not to speak of billions of years since the Fall-event, is falling.

In any case, what holds true is that the loan of the Eternal to a renegade who wanted to show Him, the Eternal, that he could do it better, has expired.

This time was the beginning of time. The end of time is now at the door of all nations and all people. Time is simply time, which at some point runs out.

Indeed, on all continents the world is falling victim to the "over." "Over" means: There is no more inflow of energy. The world, however one may call it, is time. Time has run out—it is over. It is finished. What is being hyped up here and there as a catch-up model is nothing more than sham. Any action for the sake of action is an illusion.

Neither wealth nor other great assets, neither fighting nor dispute are of any use. It is over!

Neither religions nor priests, nor sacraments and tabernacles are of any use—all rites and cults are passing away. It is over!

Of use would have been living step-by-step the Ten Commandments of God given by Moses and also the Sermon on the Mount of Jesus of Nazareth, which are excerpts from the primordial eternal law of the love for God and neighbor.

Hope is merely a remnant of what once was, like a river or even the ocean, which dries up and disappears, along with many kinds of marine life, etc., etc. It is over.

The New Age, also called the New Era, stands under the flag of seven princely pairs, guardians of the law of infinity. They will initiate the New Era in due time, the time that will lead into eternity through the appearance of the Christ of God, who as Jesus of Nazareth promised the people: I come soon!

The time of the Christ of God is rising very gradually, for in the very basis of the planet Earth, a spiritual, fine-material part, directly from the Sanctum of the eternal Being, is stirring more and more, to rise up and change the Earth.

Despite all the upheavals that take place on the Earth beforehand, there will still exist here and there parts of the Earth that will serve the sinful human race for expiation, because the guilt, the burden of many souls and people, is immeasurable.

In the Earth and in higher atmospheres of the Earth, the divine Wisdom prepares the coming of the Christ of God.

This time of preparation includes, among other things, the wake-up calls to turn back and return home to the eternal Father's house, the home-bringing to the Kingdom of Peace.

The teaching will be the peace that means:
God, the peace, the love for God and neighbor in you, and you, O human child and soul-being,

in God, the love for God and neighbor. The time is approaching for the Kingdom of Peace.

The supporting pair of the divine Wisdom has been working in the spirit of the Christ of God. Whether still in this world or from the Kingdom of God, the Wisdom in God stands for the coming of the Christ of God.

All seven regencies stand in this spirit:

A new heaven—a new peaceful Earth with beings and people in the spirit of the love for God and neighbor. And there will be peace.

In this awareness, after nearly five decades of the fullness of the heavenly word, of the I Am the I Am, and countless cosmic schoolings from the divine Wisdom, the supporting pair of the divine Wisdom takes its leave of this world.

God in us, and we in God.

A Word of Thanks from the Prophetess and Emissary of God

A Word of Thanks from the Prophetess and Emissary of God

My name is Gabriele.

For nearly 50 years, I have been privileged to reveal the Word of the eternal God to the people and to give them an understanding of His nature, which is absolute love.

In this primordial holy word "love," I, Gabriele, the prophetess of God, allow myself to thank the seven Cherubim for their ever-present protection during these decades of the fight against the prophetic word.

In this spirit and in the name of the All-Highest, I may assuredly also thank my former teacher, Brother Emanuel, who not only instructed me in three years of training to become the prophetess of God, but who has also accompanied me over many incarnations since Jesus of Nazareth.

As I was allowed to learn, he is the Cherub of divine Wisdom, just as I am the Seraph of the third basic power, his spirit dual.

In the name of the All-Highest, a deep and profound thank you to my spiritual teacher, about whom I was privileged to learn is my dual.

Dear brothers and dear sisters of the Eternal Being, Cherubim and Seraphim and all the beings of light, I thank you for your support, for your help, for the heartbeat, which I, too, may be in the Kingdom of God, in the kingdom of love.

Eternal Father, kind, merciful God, to You and to Your Son a deep and profound thank you for the growing awareness: The eternal homeland is present.

A deep thank you to the brothers and sisters, the Cherubim and Seraphim. Time ripens, the path of incarnation grows ever shorter. I am going home.

In deep respect before my divine brother, the Christ of God, who as Jesus of Nazareth endured the whole disaster, up to the last breath in the "It is Finished."

Brother, beloved brother, you gave the divine Wisdom the mission to prepare the way for Your return and to complete this faithfully.

We gave our promise, and it will be.

Then it is done.

Everything is again pure, clean, noble.

That is also our life, and that is how it will continue—eternally.

In joyful thankfulness,
one with the Cherub of divine Wisdom

To this word of thanks from the prophetess and emissary of God, a brother wrote the following letter to Gabriele:

Dear Gabriele,
Never have I heard a more profound devotion to the highest being of the Being, a humbler greatness, than in your words, so full of warmth, humility and the deepest communion with our primordial homeland.

Such unity and love speaks from it all, that one wants only to take the most direct path home.

In each word, one can feel that you live in the eternal Being and persevere in this cold world for the sake of the mission.

What thanks are due to you, you, who have borne everything in this hostile world, in order to be able to say in very simple words about this mighty, all-encompassing mission of the Christ of God to the supporting pair of the divine Wisdom: "And it will be"?

Dear Gabriele, I thank you for the path of love that is our way home, which you have brought to everyone, which you live and personify as an example, and for allowing us to share in your heavenly nature.

With all my heart: Thank you!
Martin

God-Father,
the Eternal All-One,
Reveals His Word
through his Emissary
of the Present Time

God-Father, the Eternal All-One, Reveals His Word through His Emissary of the Present Time

*T*he eternal Being, the law of God, the I Am, does not have the language of human beings. In the prophetic word, My word is the following:

In the consciousness of the "Let there be," the four natures of God emerge from the seven regencies, Order, Will, Wisdom and Earnestness. In the name of the Almighty eternal All-One God, they take up the four trumpets that stand before them and apply them. The calls of the trumpets give the word of the Eternal to His sons and daughters—and to the domineering ones of this world, who do not want to believe that time is running out according to conditional parameters.

The call of the trumpets, the heavenly word, sounds out in the mother tongue of an instrument.

My sons and My daughters, I, the Eternal, call you for the last time to turn back and return home to the eternal Father's house.

The time of the personal devastation of your souls and the devastation of the Earth has reached its high point. The libidinousness, the robbing, plundering, murdering and killing, everything that people have still devised in the way of cruelty and applied to their fellow human beings, is over. The noose around the neck, which every power-hungry person has braided for himself, he also tightens himself.

The air is running out, the heart of the Earth is beating less and less. The harvest is due, just as the bestial egomania dealt with its human brothers and human sisters, as well as with the animal and plant world.

This materialistic Earth is dying and with it also the causers and the perpetrators of the countless crimes against the law of life.

The Earth will be empty, the land, the fields, forests and trees will decay.

What is left over?

Who is left over?

Only the one who was and is like the state of the Earth will be.

The calls of the trumpets call the sons and daughters of God to turn back and to follow the path that leads to Me, the I Am the I Am.

In this spirit, the trumpets continue
to sound out.
His word resounds over the Earth.

The Christ of God prepares His coming.

Under the sign of the lily—Sophia—His words continue to apply: "I come soon: no priests, no pastors, no cassock-wearers of any kind, no churches, no cathedrals."

I Am who I Am, in you, My son, and in you, My daughter, and you in Me, the Eternal All-One, and there will be peace.

Follow the path; come back to the kingdom of eternity.

You are not invited, because since the primordial beginning, you are My children, My sons and daughters.

I Am who I Am, the Father-Mother-God.

Epilogue

Dear reader, after these shattering and deeply impressing words, a few comments on the subject:

The Eternal Kingdom, God, the Eternal, and the Prince of Wisdom have given the final signal for an epochal change in this world.

It is as it is. Yet it need not have been.

At the end of a four-thousand-year cycle of the prophetesses and prophets of God, of the messengers from the Eternal Kingdom, heaven was once again wide open as never before in the history of humankind. For nearly five decades, the whole truth from the Kingdom of God has poured out of the cornucopia of divine Wisdom onto this Earth. The regency pair of Wisdom taught in all facets the Christ-God-path of redemption and homebringing of all fallen souls and people into the Eternal Kingdom. Countless revelations, schoolings and concrete help for a life according to the Commandments of God of the love for God and neighbor for all situations of life on Earth have been given to all people of good will.

The Eternal Kingdom has given everything, so that the people can turn back and not fall into the abyss toward which the world was heading. From the very beginning, the Eternal Kingdom has shown the threatening abyss that will swallow the world, if the people do not turn back and change their ways, but continue to pay homage to the religious transfer of the Fall that is leading the world into ruin with the help of the state powerful who are servile to it, with its creed of hellish damnation and ruin, death and violence against human beings, nature and animals, indeed, against the whole Mother Earth.

Again and again, the Eternal Kingdom has explained that nature and Mother Earth will rise up and shake off their tormentors, the human beings, because soon, they will no longer be able to bear their iniquity, crime and destruction. God, the Eternal, has thus, time and again, given warning in good time of the consequences, which, according to the iron law of cause and effect, will inevitably come upon humankind if the people do not turn back and change their ways.

If the people had listened to the word of God through the mouth of a prophet, much could still have been prevented or mitigated.

So that the people would not learn about the elucidation and truth from the Eternal Kingdom, church and state power immediately took action, when nearly five decades ago, the Kingdom of God directed His word to the people through His prophetess. They proceeded in the tradition of Baalistic models of the cults of idols and priests, which had already slandered and persecuted the prophets of God of the Old Covenant as well as Jesus of Nazareth, and many times, had them murdered with the help of the state powerful.

In our time, it is the force of the two-sword alliance of church and state power under the leading sword of the church, anchored in the Vatican ecclesiastical dogma, which from the beginning, persecuted the Eternal Word and the prophetess of God with all means and then, when both could neither co-opt nor defeat them, ensured, through their means of power, wealth and false testimony, that the word of God was boycotted and hushed up.

From the very beginning, the priestly cults have also made use of servile state representatives for their fight against the word of God and His prophetess. Until today, cult and state authorities from many countries including Germany, publicly pay homage to the despot of the two swords before his throne in his palace in Rome.

The result of this alliance of the force of the sword was and is until today: slander and persecution of the word and of the prophetess of God, then hushed up—and now, climate collapse.

For decades, every warning about the catastrophic consequences for this world of the despotism of the two swords under the leadership of the church, especially for Mother Earth and nature, was met with scorn and derision from the palaces of the churches and heads of state.

Now that the catastrophe has set in and can no longer be denied, one hears from there pious and concerned slogans and nice speeches. But this does not change anything about the following fact:

All those who have contributed to the fact that the word of God has been suppressed and withheld from the people have thereby burdened themselves with a tremendous soul guilt. By spreading the word of truth from the Eternal Kingdom, millions upon millions of people could still have heard and followed the message of peace and of the love for God and neighbor toward people, nature and animals. They could have changed their lives and turned back. This would have spared not only many people but also the animals and nature tremendous suffering, and the consequences of the climate change could have been mitigated.

All the suffering that could have been prevented now weighs on the souls of all those in the church and state power who contributed to preventing the dissemination of the message from the Kingdom of God through the mouth of a prophet.

Now, the heavens are closing again. The consequences of the law of cause and effect, of sowing and reaping, are becoming evident in full measure. The Earth will be a desert, a planet of expiation for this sinful human race. This means incarnations upon incarnations in the wheel of reincarnation on the climate-collapsing Earth.

It is important to repeatedly point out who is largely to blame for this. Church and state representatives still believe that they can deceive the people with concerned and seemingly wise slogans about the so-called climate change, which, in reality, is already the climate catastrophe into which, if nothing else, they have plunged the world. These are ineffectual diversionary maneuvers, because churches and church-favorable state representatives are still propelling the climate catastrophe forward with their cult dogmatic that despises life and animals.

The war of extermination against nature and animals is still raging as before; leading the way is the daily clerically sanctioned millionfold massacre of animals, the killing orgies of the butchers for the satisfaction of the palate in animal cannibalism.

Again and again, the Eternal Kingdom has warned and admonished especially against the consequences of the criminal iniquity against the kingdoms of nature and the animals.

Already more than two decades ago, on February 27, 2001, God, the Eternal, spoke in His word of revelation:

Should human beings again toss My words to the wind, the storm, the fate that is worldwide, will begin and sweep away the people by the hundreds of thousands—on the one hand, through worldwide catastrophes, on the other, through illnesses which break in over them like the epidemics, which, by turning their backs on every kind of spiritual ethics and morals, they have inflicted on the animals ...

Church and a church-favorable state have made sure that also this and other similar admonitions of the Eternal were suppressed and tossed to the wind.

That is why we are experiencing today what God, the Eternal, wanted to safeguard humankind from. What is taking place now is what the Kingdom of God has foretold through the mouth of a prophet for five decades, in the event that humankind does not turn back and change its ways.

And let it be said, once more: The responsible persons in church and state, who suppressed the word of God, relegated it to the wind and persecuted the bearer of His word, have thereby loaded a heavy soul-guilt on themselves. It would be better for them if they had never been born.

The passage of time has exposed the two-sword alliance of church and state power; the word of God is being fulfilled with regard to this world in the sad truth that the word of God was tossed to the wind, that the seed has sprouted under the leadership of the Baal regime and its power commissioners, and that the world has fallen into the abyss.

Even science today consistently predicts further catastrophic developments due to the change of the world climate. Thereby forecasts like the one published in the *Frankfurter Rundschau* (The Frankfurt Review) on August 20, 2020, "*Until 2100 a devastating hot time threatens as a result of the climate change,*" is still one of the positive predictions. In its report, the newspaper refers to the study by an international team of researchers led by the Dutchman Marten Scheffer of Wageningen University based on assumptions made by the Intergovernmental Panel on Climate Change (IPCC).

There are also significantly more pessimistic predictions. Thus, we can read in the magazine *Focus* of October 2019: *"Shock prognosis to the climate catastrophe: In the middle of the century, humankind is at an end."* This is the conclusion of a report by the Australian Breakthrough National Centre for Climate Restoration, which has received much attention worldwide.

There is much speculation about how quickly and to what extent the catastrophe progresses. Even today, no one seriously believes that this trend can still be reversed; on the contrary—because so far, it has not even been possible to stop it. And in the opinion of many scientists, the time that would have remained for the world to do so has also already run out.

No matter how you look at it—there is nothing that can be put forward against the clear word from the Eternal Kingdom. For this world, as we have experienced it until now, what holds true is: It is over.